Play Cribbage *to Win*

Dan Barlow

Sterling Publishing Co., Inc.
New York

Edited by Claire Bazinet

Library of Congress Cataloging-in-Publication Data

Barlow, Dan
  Play cribbage to win / by Dan Barlow.
    p. cm
  Includes index.
  ISBN 0-8069-4313-0
    1. Cribbage. I. Title.

  GV1295.C9 B27 2000
  795.41'1—dc21

                                        00-033902

10 9 8 7 6 5 4 3 2

Published by Sterling Publishing Company, Inc.
387 Park Avenue South, New York, N.Y. 10016
© 2000 by Dan Barlow
Distributed in Canada by Sterling Publishing
^c/o Canadian Manda Group, One Atlantic Avenue, Suite 105
Toronto, Ontario, Canada M6K 3E7
Distributed in Great Britain by Chrysalis Books
64 Brewery Road, London N7 9NT England
Distributed in Australia by Capricorn Link (Australia) Pty Ltd.
P.O. Box 6651, Baulkham Hills, Business Centre, NSW 2153, Australia
Manufactured in the United States of America

Sterling ISBN 0-8069-4313-0

For Jennifer, my partner

Contents

Introduction

The game of cribbage was invented by Sir John Suckling (1609-1642), a British Royalist who frequented the court of King Charles I. Suckling was one of the so-called "Cavalier Poets," and it's common today to find one or two of his poems in English Literature textbooks. Cribbage, however, may prove to be Sir John's most significant contribution to the world, for the game is widely played in all English-speaking countries, and is regarded by many as the best two-handed card game.

This book will teach you the rules and the strategy of cribbage. If you've never played before, the game may seem a bit complicated at first, but stick with it. I promise you'll soon find it to be a very simple game which, although chance plays its part, requires enough skill to catch and keep your interest.

If you're a knowledgeable or experienced player, you may simply want to give the rules a quick review or skip over them entirely and go straight for the strategy sections. Here you'll find pointers on discarding and pegging, quizzes to keep you on your toes, and expert tips for taking your game to the highest level. You'll also learn about the American Cribbage Congress, an organization that runs cribbage tournaments and cribbage clubs throughout the U.S.A.

No cribbage player is skillful enough to win every game —no one even comes close. A great many games—perhaps the majority—are won by the player who is simply luckier. But the more tactics you add to your arsenal, the more challenging and satisfying you will find the game to be. Hence this book.

No, you don't actually need to study and memorize this book in order to enjoy cribbage. It's a game that's fun at any skill level. But winning at cribbage *is* more fun than losing at cribbage, and this book is designed to soon have you winning more than your fair share.

The Cribbage Board

To play the a two-handed game of cribbage, you'll need an opponent, of course, and also some equipment: a deck of cards, four pegs, and a cribbage board.

Cribbage boards are available in several styles. The basic cribbage board has two pair of 30-hole "streets," divided into groups of five holes for ease in counting, which run along the length of each side. During play, the players each move their pegs up their outside street, down their inside street, back up again on the outside, and back down again on the inside (commonly called the 4th street), and then finally into a "game hole." The "long" cribbage board consists of 60 holes up and back on each side. Other boards may spiral or snake their way to the end, or may be circular.

Basic Cribbage Board

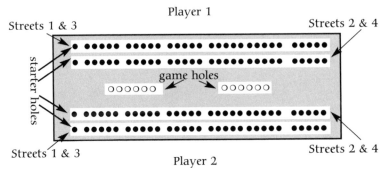

Boards come in various price ranges, and most boards include a set of pegs inside a storage compartment. Some may also have storage for a deck of cards. Any board will do, so long as it allows you to count to 121 points.

Rules of Play

The game of cribbage is a race around a pegboard, the winner being the player who first scores 121 points. A standard deck of cards is used. Movement around the cribbage board is simple: whenever a player scores any points, he lifts up his rear peg and jumps it over his front peg the proper number of holes.

Each cribbage hand is divided into three separate parts:

1. Dealing and discarding

2. Playing of the hand

3. Scoring the points in the hands and crib

Dealing and Discarding To begin play, the players cut the deck, and the player who cuts the lowest card (ace is low) deals the first hand. The deal alternates thereafter.

Each player receives six cards, and chooses two of them to discard, facedown, into the "crib." This "toss" leaves each player with a four-card hand, and creates a third four-card hand (the crib).

The crib and the deck should be placed on the dealer's side of the board, so there is no argument over who dealt the hand. After each player has discarded to the crib, the non-dealer cuts the remaining deck and the dealer turns up the top card. This card is the "starter" or "cut" card. If the starter card is a jack, the dealer immediately scores two points.

Playing the Hand The play of the hand begins as the non-dealer selects one of his cards, lays it down in front of him, and announces its "count." If a 7 is played, he says "seven." If it's an ace, he says "one." If any face card is played, the count is "ten."

The dealer next plays a card by placing it before him and announcing the "new" count, determined by adding the face value of his own card to the current count. For example, if the count from the previous play is 7 and the dealer plays a queen, the new count of "seventeen" is announced. The non-dealer then plays again and announces the next new count. Play continues until both players have played all four of their cards.

During play, the count can never go higher than 31. If a player cannot play a card without sending the count over 31, he says "go," at which point the opponent must continue playing until he, too, cannot make a legal play. The count then reverts to zero and play begins again (with the player first saying "go" playing first in the new cycle).

During the play of each cribbage hand, points are scored as follows:

1. Making the count 15 (2 points).

2. Making the count 31 (2 points).

3. Playing the last card, in a cycle that does not reach exactly 31 (1 point).

4. Playing the second consecutive card of any rank— i.e., an opponent plays a 4, and you play a 4 of your own—or you play two consecutive 4's, opponent having said "go" between them (2 points).

5. Playing the third consecutive card of any rank (6 points).

6. Playing the fourth consecutive card of any rank (12 points).

7. Creating a "run"—i.e., three or more cards in sequence (1 point for each card in the sequence).

Here are three hands to illustrate.

1.

Bob	Pat	
10	5 (15 for 2)	Pat scores 2 points for making the count 15.
5 (20 for 2)	K (30)	Bob scores 2 points for pairing Pat's 5.
Go	A (31 for 2)	Bob has no legal play; Pat makes the count 31, scoring 2.
4	4 (8 for 2)	Pat scores 2 points for pairing Bob's 4.
7 (15 for 3)		Bob scores 2 points for making the count 15, *and* 1 more point for playing the last card in a cycle that did not reach exactly 31.

Bob's total: 5

Pat's total: 6

2.

Ed	Jo	
7	4 (11)	
4 (15 for 4)	4 (19 for 6)	Ed scores 2 points for making the count 15, *and* 2 more points for pairing Jo's 4; Jo scores 6 points for playing the third consecutive 4.
6 (25)	6 (31 for 4)	Jo scores 2 points for making the count 31, *and* 2 more for pairing Ed's 6.
2	5 (7 for 1)	Jo scores 1 point for playing the last card in a cycle that did not reach exactly 31.

Ed's total: 4

Jo's total: 11

3.

Ann	Sue	
A (1)	7 (8)	
2 (10)	5 (15 for 2)	Sue scores 2 points for making the count 15.

| 3 (18) | 4 (22 for 4) | Sue scores 4 points for creating a 4-card run (2-3-4-5) |
| 6 (28 for 7) | 2 (30 for 6) | Ann scores 7 points for creating a seven-card run (A-2-3-4-5-6-7); Sue scores 5 points for creating a five-card run (the last five cards played were 2-3-4-5-6), *and* one more point for playing the last card in a cycle that did not reach exactly 31. |

Ann's total: 7

Sue's total: 12

Scoring the Points in the Hands and Crib After both players have played their four cards, the non-dealer counts and pegs the points in his hand. If the game hole (121) is reached, he is the winner, and the dealer does not get to count his points. If the non-dealer does not reach the game hole, the dealer then counts and pegs the points in his hand. Finally, the *dealer* counts and pegs the points that are in the crib.

When counting points, *the starter card becomes a fifth card in each of the three hands.* Points are scored as follows:

1. Any card combination that totals 15 (6-9, 4-5-6, 3-3-4-5, A-2-3-4-5, etc.) is worth 2 points. The ace has a value of 1, each face card has a value of 10; thus A-4-K adds up to 15, and is worth 2 points.

2. Any pair is worth 2 points. Three of a kind (which is actually three separate pairs) is worth 6 points.

Four of a kind (six separate pairs) is worth 12 points.

3. Any run (three or more consecutive cards) is worth 1 point for each card in the run. Thus, 3-4-5 is worth 3 points, A-2-3-4 is worth 4 points, and 9-10-J-Q-K is worth 5 points. The ace is always low, thus Q-K-A is not a legal run.

4. Four cards of the same suit *in one's hand* (a flush) is worth 4 points. If the starter card is also the same suit, an additional point is scored. However, to score points for a flush *in the crib*, all four cards *and* the starter card must be of the same suit.

5. The jack of the same suit as the starter card is worth 1 point. Remember, if the starter card *itself* is a jack, the dealer receives two points when the starter card is turned up. This is called the right jack, or his nobs.

We've seen that A-4-K is worth 2 points, but what about A-4-4-K? This is worth 6 points: 2 for the pair of 4's, 2 for A-4-K (15), and 2 for the *second* A-4-K (15). By substituting one 4 for another, we create a second combination that totals 15. If the starter card happened to be a 4 as well, the hand (A-4-4-4-K) would be worth 12 points: 6 for the three 4's, and 6 for the three A-4-K combinations, each of which adds up to 15.

This "substituting" of one card for another works with runs as well as 15-2's. Suppose your hand is A-2-2-3 and the starter card is a 3. How many points do you have? The answer is 15. The three deuces are worth 6 points. Each A-2-3 run is worth 3 points, and there are 3 such runs. There are no card combinations that add up to 15.

Starting on the next page, let's look at several sample hands and their values. Assume that none of the hands given is a flush.

Your Hand	Cut	Value	Explanation	
4–5–6–Q	Q	11	Q–5 (15)	2 points
			Q–5 (15)	2 points
			4–5–6 (15)	2 points
			Q–Q (pair)	2 points
			4–5–6 (run)	3 points

The 5 is involved in three 15-2's, one with each queen, and one with the 4-6.

Your Hand	Cut	Value	Explanation	
6–7–7–8	7	21	7–8 (15)	2 points
			7–8 (15)	2 points
			7–8 (15)	2 points
			7–7–7 (3 7's)	6 points
			6–7–8 (run)	3 points
			6–7–8 (run)	3 points
			6–7–8 (run)	3 points

Each of the three 7's is involved in a 15-2 with the 8, and each of the three 7's is involved in a run with the 6-8.

Your Hand	Cut	Value	Explanation	
3–3–3–6	9	16	6–9 (15)	2 points
			3–3–9 (15)	2 points
			3–3–9 (15)	2 points
			3–3–9 (15)	2 points
			3–3–3–6 (15)	2 points
			3–3–3 (3 3's)	6 points

Note that there are three different 3-3-9 combinations when holding 3-3-3-9.

Your Hand	Cut	Value	Explanation	
5-5-6-J	5	14	J-5 (15)	2 points
			J-5 (15)	2 points
			J-5 (15)	2 points
			5-5-5 (15)	2 points
			5-5-5 (3 5's)	6 points

Note that if the jack is the same suit as the cut, this hand is worth 15 points.

Your Hand	Cut	Value	Explanation	
A-4-5-6	4	14	4-5-6 (15)	2 points
			4-5-6 (15)	2 points
			A-4-4-6 (15)	2 points
			4-5-6 (run)	3 points
			4-5-6 (run)	3 points
			4-4 (pair)	2 points

If the A-4-5-6 in your hand were all the same suit, this hand would be worth 18 points.

Some hands are tricky, but most are not. If you systematically count your 15-2's, then your pairs, then your runs, then your flush, then the right jack, you should become adept at finding all of your points. Experience will help. There are only so many possible hands, and eventually you'll have seen most of them.

By the way, you will probably find it more efficient to count your runs and pairs together, when the card that is paired is also part of the run. For instance, the hand 2-2-3-4 can be seen as a pair and two three-card runs. It can also be seen as a "double-run," which is worth 8 points. A four-card double-run (8-9-10-10-J) is worth 10 points (a pair and two four-card runs). A "triple-run" (A-2-2-2-3) is worth 15 points (three three-card runs and three of a kind), and a "double-double run" (A-A-2-3-3) is worth 16 points (four three-card runs and two pairs). These multiple-run hands will be worth even more, of course, if they also include 15-2's or the right jack.

> **NOTE**
> In order to simplify and save space in the following quiz, and elsewhere throughout the book, the suits of the cards are not given—but when the suits are relevant, *cards of the same suit are underlined.*

Quiz 1

On the next pages, you will find a number of cribbage hands. Some are common, some are fairly rare. Many of them are tricky. Try to determine the value of each. This will be especially good practice for you if you aren't an experienced player.

In doing the quizzes in this book, you may wish to use a deck of cards, if the rows of numbers and letters given make visualizing the hands difficult for you. For this first quiz only, however, we are supplying the "cards" to help you become familiar with the space-saving method of card notation. The correct values of the hands (the solutions) to this first quiz may be found on page 22, along with explanations.

Hand	Cut	Value	Cut	Hand
1. 3-3-4-5	Q	___		
2. A-A-7-7	8	___		

Hand	Cut	Value	Cut	Hand
3. 4-5-6-7	4	___		
4. A-2-3-9	3	___		
5. A-A-6-7	7	___		
6. 4-4-5-6	6	___		
7. 2-2-3-4	8	___		
8. 5-5-5-2	3	___		
9. J-J-Q-K	5	___		
10. 2-3-4-6	6	___		
11. 6-7-7-9	8	___		
12. 4-4-7-7	4	___		
13. 2-2-2-9	2	___		
14. 3-4-4-4	8	___		
15. A-2-3-J	2	___		
16. A-2-3-4	9	___		

Hand	Cut	Value	Cut	Hand
17. 5-J-Q-K	5	___		
18. A-2-3-J	Q	___		
19. 2-4-6-8	K	___		
20. 5-5-5-J	5	___		
21. 4-5-5-6	5	___		
22. A-7-7-7	7	___		
23. 3-3-3-4	5	___		
24. 7-7-8-8	9	___		
25. 2-2-3-4	4	___		
26. J-J-J-Q	K	___		
27. 4-5-6-J	5	___		
28. A-3-4-7	4	___		
29. A-6-7-8	A	___		
30. 3-3-9-9	9	___		

Solutions–Quiz 1

1. 12 points (two 15-2's, and a double run)
2. 12 points (four 15-2's, and two pairs)
3. 16 points (three 15-2's, and a 4-card double run)
4. 18 points (three 15-2's, a double run, and a flush)
5. 12 points (four 15-2's, and two pairs)
6. 24 points (four 15-2's, and a double-double run)
7. 12 points (two 15-2's, and a double run)
8. 14 points (four 15-2's, and three of a kind)
9. 17 points (four 15-2's, a double run, the right jack)
10. 15 points (three 15-2's, one pair, 3-card run, flush)
11. 16 points (three 15-2's, and a 4-card double run)
12. 20 points (six 15-2's, one pair, and three of a kind)
13. 20 points (four 15-2's, and four of a kind)
14. 14 points (four 15-2's, and three of a kind)
15. 15 points (three 15-2's, a double run, the right jack)
16. 12 points (two 15-2's, one 4-card run, 4-card flush)
17. 21 points (six 15-2's, one pair, 3-card run, flush)
18. 13 points (two 15-2's, run, 5-flush, the right jack)
19. 0 points (A hand of no points is often referred to as a "19 hand" because 19 is the one impossible score below 25.)
20. 29 points (eight 15-2's, four of a kind, right jack)
21. 23 points (four 15-2's, and a triple run)
22. 24 points (six 15-2's, and four of a kind)
23. 21 points (three 15-2's, and a triple run)
24. 24 points (four 15-2's, and a double-double run)
25. 18 points (one 15-2, and a double-double run)
26. 16 points (triple run, and the right jack)
27. 20 points (four 15-2's, double run, and a flush)
28. 12 points (three 15-2's, one pair, four-card flush)
29. 17 points (four 15-2's, one pair, run, and a flush)
30. 14 points (three 15-2's, one pair, three of a kind)

Getting the Point?

You may have gotten the impression here that a cribbage hand tends to average about 15 or 20 points. Actually, the average is much lower. But if you can see the points in the hands here, you should have little trouble seeing the points in smaller hands.

By the way, the counting of points is the one aspect of cribbage that involves no strategy. You have a certain number of points, and you peg them. If you fail to notice all of your points, and peg fewer than you deserve, you lose the points you missed (unless your opponent is feeling generous). Your opponent is under no obligation to help you count your points; in fact, in some circles your opponent is entitled to any points you miss, assuming he spots them (this rule, called "muggins," is optional).

Clearly it is to your advantage to become adept at finding all of the points in any hand, not only because you don't want to lose any points to which you're entitled, but also because deciding which cards to toss to the crib will be much easier once you're familiar with the card combinations that have the greatest value.

When the dealer has pegged the points in his hand and his crib, the hand is over. The full deck is shuffled, and the next hand is dealt. The game ends when one player pegs into the game hole (121).

A victory by more than 30 holes is referred to as a "skunk," and is usually considered two wins. This can add interest to a game that is not especially close.

Strategy in Tossing
to the Crib

Now that you are confident you can count the points in any hand, the best strategy of tossing to the crib may seem obvious: *keep the four cards that give you the most points*. This is sometimes a good plan, but not always!

Before tossing, there are three items to consider:

1. The crib

2. The cut

3. The position

The Crib When tossing to the crib, it's a good idea to consider which player is going to be scoring the points in the crib. If you dealt the hand, it's your crib, so why not toss in something useful, like a pair, two cards that add up to 15, or two "touching" cards (cards such as 3-4 or 9-10, which might work to form a run)? This may cost you a few points in your hand, but you hope your loss is more than offset by gains in your crib. Holding 2-4-5-6-8-9, you can save 4-5-6-9, the most points possible. But the 8-9, tossed into your crib, may lead to a bigger payoff than 2-8. 8-9 will form a run if the cut or opponent's toss includes a 7 or a 10. Your opponent could toss 6-10, and the cut could be a 9, giving you a 12-point crib, where a toss of 2-8 would have given you only five points.

When it's your *opponent's* crib, you may find that keeping the most points possible leaves you tossing something useful to the enemy. If you have an excellent hand, such as 7-7-8-8, you will not hesitate to give your opponent 5-Q, painful as that may be. But suppose you hold A-2-3-5-Q-

K. The most points you can save is five (A-2-3-Q, or A-2-3-K), but this leaves you tossing 5-K or 5-Q into your opponent's crib. Clearly, keeping 2-3-5-Q is better. It costs you a point, but tossing A-K is less likely to help your opponent.

You can't always toss something good into your own crib, and you can't always avoid tossing something good into your opponent's crib. But when you have a choice, ownership of the crib is usually the deciding factor in determining which cards to toss.

> **EXPERT TIP** One often tosses touching cards in one's own crib in hopes of forming a run, but many a player will toss Q–K from a hand such as 3–4–5–10–Q–K. In fact, the 10–Q is a better toss. Either way you need a jack to form a run, but tossing 10–Q gives you a shot at a run (or even a double run) *without* a jack. Your opponent could toss a 10 (or even 8–10), and the cut could be a 9. If you've tossed Q–K, you'll be sorry.

Quiz 2

Which two cards would you toss from each of the following hands, early in the game, if it's your crib? Which would you toss, if it's your opponent's crib? Underlined cards are the same suit.

Your Hand	**Toss (to self)**	**Toss (to opponent)**
1. A-2-3-8-9-J	____	____
2. A-2-5-7-9-K	____	____
3. A-5-7-7-J-K	____	____
4. 2-5-8-9-Q-K	____	____
5. 5-6-6-J-J-K	____	____
6. 5-6-7-8-8-9	____	____

Solutions

1. Toss 8-9 to yourself, 8-J to your opponent. You don't want to give your opponent touching cards if you can avoid it, as he'll score a run more easily.
2. Toss 5-K to yourself, 2-7 to opponent.
3. Toss 5-J (or 7-7) to yourself, and J-K (or A-K) to your opponent. Tossing J-K to an opponent is risky, in that he might toss 5-Q, but keeping the A-7-7 gives you a chance at a 12-hand, by cutting a 7. Decisions like this are what make cribbage fascinating, and what give cribbage players ulcers.
4. Toss 8-9 in your own crib, and 2-8 in opponent's. 2-8 is slightly better than 2-9, because 2-8 matches up with a 5, and opponent usually hangs onto his 5's, as they usually fit with more than one of his other cards.
5. Toss 6-6 to yourself, toss 6-K to opponent. If you're willing to sacrifice two points, you might toss J-K to opponent, hoping to cut a 4. Odds are you won't get your cut, but if you desperately need a big hand, or you're feeling lucky, feel free to gamble.
6. Toss 5-6 to yourself, 5-9 to opponent.

The Cut Cribbage would be so much easier if you had psychic powers, and could determine the cut in advance. But since you don't know what the cut will be, you don't know for sure which four cards will give you the most points.

Suppose you are dealt 2-3-3-3-6-Q. What do you save? 3-3-3-6 is worth 8 points, 2-3-3-3 is worth 6. But what will the cut be? Only a 3, 6, or 9 will improve 3-3-3-6. And a 3 is highly unlikely to be cut. 2-3-3-3 will work better on the cut of an ace, a 4, a 7, or any face card.

Sometimes there are two different ways to save the most points possible. Imagine you must toss from 3-6-7-8-8-9. Would you rather hold onto 6-7-8-8 or 7-8-8-9? Each is worth 12 points, and each has the potential of improving greatly on the cut of a 6, 7, 8, or 9. 6-7-8-8 improves slightly on the cut of a 5, while 7-8-8-9 improves slightly on the cut of a 10. The difference is that 6-7-8-8 also improves on the cut of an ace or a deuce.

The lesson: if you don't care which cards you toss, think about the potential of the hand; usually you'll want to save the four cards that will give you the most points on the most cuts.

Quiz 3

Which two cards would you toss from each of the following hands, *based on their potential?* Underlined cards are the same suit.

Your Hand	Toss
1. A-2-2-3-3-7	____
2. 4-4-5-6-6-J	____
3. 3-6-6-6-6-9	____
4. 4-5-6-J-Q-K	____
5. 2-3-4-J-Q-K	____
6. 3-6-7-8-9-J	____

Solutions

1. 3-7. Keeping A-2-2-3 is better if the cut is any ten-card. A-2-3-3 is better only if the cut is a 6 or a 9.
2. 6-J. Keeping 4-4-5-6 gets you two extra points if the cut is an ace, deuce, or 7. 4-5-6-6 gets you two extra points only if the cut is a 3 or a 9.
3. 3-9. You can't do better than keeping 6-6-6-6, no matter what starter card is cut.
4. 4-6. You won't be disappointed with 5-J-Q-K, unless the cut is a 4 or a 6.
5. Q-K. Keeping 2-3-4-J is best on most cuts.

6. 9-J. If a 9 comes up you'll be sorry, but if a 3, 4, or 5 comes up, you get an extra three or four points if you've saved the flush, and you'll also end up with more on most other cuts.

The Position The position of your pegs on the board can have a major effect on your pegging strategy, as we'll see later, but can also affect your toss, especially in three cases:

1. When the cut and the crib are irrelevant.
2. When the dealer will lose if he doesn't peg out.
3. When the non-dealer needs a specific number of points to have any chance.

Let's take each of these cases one by one.

1. When the cut and the crib are irrelevant. Sometimes there's no need to consider the cut or the crib. Suppose both players are one hole from victory. Does it matter what the cut is? Not unless it's a jack, giving the dealer two points. Otherwise one player will peg out before anyone counts the points in his hand (the dealer is guaranteed at least one "go"). Does it matter how many points are in the crib? No, because someone will win before the crib is counted. In such a situation, you will retain the cards you feel are most likely to help you peg a hole before your opponent does.

What are these cards? As the non-dealer, desperately trying to prevent the dealer from pegging out, you would be well-advised to save a low card for your opening lead. This will prevent the dealer from scoring a 15-2. For both players, it helps to save a diversity of cards. You want to have several options whenever it's your turn to play. If the opening lead is a 3, the dealer will not be happy if he's holding 2-2-4-4. He is more likely to survive if he has saved 2-4-6-8.

2. When the dealer will lose if he doesn't peg out. Occasionally you will reach a position in which the dealer has no hope of winning other than to peg out. If the non-dealer has enough points to win (or the dealer *believes* this to be true), the dealer will try to peg out to prevent the non-dealer from counting those points. In such a situation, the dealer has no incentive to save any points, but will save the cards which give him his *best* chance of pegging.

What are those cards? A dealer's best bet is often to hang onto pairs or "touching" cards, which may turn into runs, as these can sometimes lead to big pegging counts.

For example:

Opponent	You
Q	5 (15-2)
Q (25)	2 (27)
Go	3 (30)
	A (31-5)

Opponent	You
6	9 (15-2)
9 (24-2)	Go
4 (28)	
2 (30-1)	10
	J (20)
	Q (30-4)

These examples show the dealer scoring runs with no help from the opponent, thanks to his touching cards. Hanging onto pairs can also work well. If the count is 29, and your opponent says, "go," you'll be pleased to be holding a pair of aces. It's nice when your opponent gets trapped into a run, or plays a card you can pair, but it's also lucky. Holding "touchers," pairs, and even 15-2's gives you an extra chance at pegging out.

What should the non-dealer be saving, when the dealer needs to peg five or six holes? Diversity is again the key. You don't want to get trapped into a run or pairing a card if the dealer might triple. Thus, needing four points, you might prefer to save 3-5-7-K, rather than 3-5-6-7. If you lead with your 3, and the dealer plays a 6, can you afford to pair, knowing that if he has another 6 he wins? Can you afford to play a 5 or a 7, knowing he can score a 3-card run? You'd feel much safer if you could play a king on that 6.

3. When the non-dealer needs a specific number of points to have any chance. Sometimes you don't care which holding gives you the most points on the most cuts. Sometimes you need to gamble on a specific cut, because it's your only hope of winning.

Suppose you have first count, and need 24 points to win, but dealer needs only four. In this situation you are interested in which holding gives you a chance at 24 points, even if that chance requires a specific (and unlikely) cut. Holding 5-5-6-6-7-Q, you would normally toss 6-Q into opponent's crib, saving 5-5-6-7, which is worth eight points, not 5-5-6-6, which is worth only four points. On *most* cuts, you'll have a better hand if you save 5-5-6-7. But if you need 24 points to have any chance of winning, you should save 5-5-6-6, hoping to cut a 4. The most you can get if you save 5-5-6-7 is 17 points (by cutting a 5), and unless you are lucky enough to peg seven holes during the play of the hand, 17 will not be enough.

When you absolutely *must* have a certain number of points, save the cards that give you a chance of getting that number of points. Even a one in forty-six chance is better than no chance at all.

Quiz 4

In this next set of problems, the opponent deals—and needs only *five* points to win. You, however, need a whopping sixteen points. Your only reasonable hope is that you can go out before the dealer counts his hand and crib. *Assume that you won't peg more than three holes*, and make the toss that gives you the best chance of winning. Under-lined cards are the same suit.

Your Hand	**Toss**
1. A-2-3-7-8-8	____
2. 3-3-4-7-7-8	____
3. A-2-3-5-5-K	____
4. <u>5</u>-<u>9</u>-<u>10</u>-J-Q-Q	____
5. 5-5-5-6-6-7	____
6. 3-4-5-6-9-9	____

Solutions

1. Toss 2-3. This assures victory if you cut a 6, and gives you 14 if you cut a 7. Earlier in the game, when you weren't desperate for points, you'd have tossed A-3, which is less likely to help opponent's crib than 2-3.
2. You can't get more than 12 if you save the 7-7-8. Thus you must toss 7-8, save 3-3-4-7, and cut a 5, for 14 points. In practice, you might decide your chances are better if you hold 3-7-7-8 and try to peg four holes (after cutting a 6, 7, 8, or 9), but by the constraints of this quiz, you must toss 7-8. The three-hole limit on pegging is not entirely realistic, but it's reasonable. You can't peg with your first card, and opponent, who does not need to peg at all, will be trying his best to prevent you from pegging. To score more than a go and a 15-2 would be extremely lucky.

3. Toss the 5's. A-2-3-K gives you 14 if you cut a deuce. 3-5-5-K gives you 14 if you cut a 5. Since you are holding two 5's, and one deuce, you're more likely to cut a deuce.
4. Toss the queens, and save the flush. This wins for sure on the cut of a 5, 9, 10, or jack, and could win on the cut of a queen or king. 5-10-J-Q loses if the cut is a 9, and probably loses if the cut is a king. 5-J-Q-Q loses if the cut is a 9 or a jack.
5. 5-5-6-7 wins on the cut of a 5, 6, or 7, and gets you 14 on the cut of a 4. However, 5-5-5-6 wins on the cut of a 4, 5, or 7, and gets you 14 on the cut of any ten-card. Toss 6-7.
6. The best choices are 3-4-5-6 and 4-5-6-9. Either gives you 16 points on the cut of a 6, and 14 points on the cut of a 4 or a 5. But 3-4-5-6 also gives you 14 points on the cut of a 3. Toss the 9's.

You undoubtedly have realized that in order to solve problems such as these, you need to be able to mentally calculate the value of your possible holdings on any cut. This will be a bit time-consuming at first, but the more you play, the more efficient you'll become.

You should also have noticed that in most cases you would have held the hand differently if not for your perilous position on the board. You won't win often when you need a specific cut, but it's better to give yourself a slight chance than no chance at all.

Strategy in the Opening Plays of Hand

To win consistently, you need good cards, and you need good cuts. But in the long run, your cards should be as good as your opponent's cards. And if you make intelligent decisions when tossing to the crib, the cut should help you as often as it does your opponent (it will only *seem* like your opponent gets better cards and better cuts than you do). So does it all come down to luck?

No.

Luck is certainly a factor, but during the play of the hand, a great deal of strategy is possible, and in a close game, any play which nets you a few holes can make the difference between winning and losing. True, each player has only four cards to play, but the order in which those cards are played can be critical.

For example:

A.		**B.**	
Jeff	**Pam**	**Jeff**	**Pam**
9	6 (15–2)	3	3 (6–2)
3 (18)	3 (21–2)	9 (15–2)	4 (19)
5 (26)	4 (30–4)	4 (23–2)	6 (29)
4	2 (6–1)	Go	2 (31–2)
		5 (5–1)	

The cards are the same, but in hand A, Pam outpegs Jeff by 9 holes, while in hand B, Jeff outpegs Pam, five holes to four. A ten-hole difference on only one hand! And since a cribbage game usually consists of ten to twelve hands, it's easy to see that sound pegging tactics are vital if you are to win your share of close games.

As we look at various pegging strategies, we'll find that many are based on two general ideas:

1. There are lots of face cards (and 10's) in the deck.

2. Your opponent will try to save a good hand.

How do these ideas help us? They help us guess what an opponent has in his hand. If you could see your opponent's cards, you'd seldom get outpegged, agreed? So at the beginning of the hand, when you have nothing else to go on, consider that your opponent may have been dealt several "ten-cards." There are, after all, 16 of them in the deck. That being the case, it's clear that making the count 5 or 21 is unwise, as your opponent can easily score 15-2 or 31-2.

As the hand progresses, it may arise that your opponent does not have face cards. But since she has tried to save a good hand, once you've seen a couple of her cards, you can make an educated guess about her remaining cards. Often your guess will be wrong, because opponent will have a bad hand. But (trust me on this) if your opponent has a bad hand, you will be happy, even if she pegs a bit more than she might have.

Following, we'll examine strategies on opening lead, in responding to the opening lead, and in the remainder of the play. Then we'll look at strategies that are specific to the final stages of the game, the all-important "4th Street."

The Opening Lead

The opening lead is the first card played by the non-dealer, and while this card can never score points, it can be the most crucial card played. Choosing the opening lead needn't involve complicated thought processes, not if you develop a system of priorities. A priority system will also save time, leaving you more time to consider decisions you may have later in the play (true, there's no time limit on a specific play, but your opponent may become annoyed if you take five minutes to play every card).

Your order of priorities should be in line with the following:

- If you have a 2-3 or an ace-4 combination, lead from it. This leads to a 15-2 if opponent plays a face card. Remember, opponent often has lots of face cards, and even if she has other cards with her face cards, she may not be able to play them without offering you a run. For instance, if you lead the 4 from A-4-K-K, and opponent has 3-3-10-10, chances are she'll play a 10 rather than risk your scoring a three-card run. You then score 15-2 with your ace.

- If you have a 4-7 or a 3-9 combination, lead the lower card. This allows you to score a safe 15-2 if your opponent pairs your lead.

- Lead from three of a kind. This allows you to triple without danger, if an opponent pairs.

- Lead from a pair, hoping to triple. It is safest, of course, if your pair is higher than 7's, so that there is no danger of an opponent scoring 12 points, after you score 6 for tripling.

- With a 6-9 combination, lead the 6. If an opponent scores 15-2, you can pair his 9 safely.

- Lead from three cards that total 11. (4-4-3, for example, or 2-4-5). If your opponent keeps playing face cards, you'll score 31-2. Another opportunity to take advantage of the fact that there are a wealth of face cards in the deck.

- With a 3-6 or ace-7 combination, lead the higher card. You score 15-2 if your opponent pairs. Of course, a player who has a 6 with which to pair yours will often have a 9, and score 15-2 instead.

- Lead a face card from F-5, or the 8 from 7-8. You can pair if an opponent scores 15-2. You risk the possibility your opponent will triple after you pair, however.

- Lead a low card, hoping that your opponent can't pair, and knowing he can't score 15-2. This is a good defensive play, although it's often best to hang onto your low cards in the hope of scoring 31-2 later in the play.

The dealer, by playing second, has an advantage in the pegging game, so anything you can do on opening lead to reduce this advantage will pay off. The suggestions above are designed to set you up for future pegging, or to reduce opponent's chances of pegging.

Quiz 5

Assume it's early in the game. Which card would you lead from each of the following hands?

1. 7-7-8-8
2. 6-7-8-9
3. 2-3-K-K
4. 2-3-6-9
5. 2-7-8-9
6. 3-4-7-8
7. A-A-4-Q
8. A-6-7-8

Solutions

No solutions will always be "correct"—what works best will depend on an opponent's holding—but the following should be useful strategies:

1. Lead an 8. If it gets paired, you can triple without fear that your opponent has the fourth 8.
2. Lead the 6. If your opponent scores 15-2 you can pair safely. You'll probably get the worst of the pegging duel if you can't get out without a run starting.

3. Lead the 3. It's tempting to lead a king, hoping your opponent pairs, but he's more likely to have a 5 than a king. Unless your opponent has a 7, 8, or 9, he'll probably play a face card on your 3, giving you two points for 15-2. If you lead a king and he plays a 5, you could be outpegged by a wide margin:

You	Opponent
K	5 (15-2)
K (25)	6 (31-2)
3	5 (8)
2 (10)	4 (14-4)

You	Opponent
K	5 (15-2)
2 (17)	10 (27)
3 (30-1)	J
K (20)	Q (30-4)

4. Here the 6 and the 3 are perfectly safe; if he pegs on either, you get equal counter-pegging. But the 3 is still better, as your opponent may play a face card.
5. Lead the 8. You may need the deuce to break up a run. By keeping a diversity of cards, you have a better chance of making safe plays in the future.
6. Lead the 4. If it gets paired, you score 15-2 with your 7.
7. Lead the 4. An opponent is unlikely to pair your ace, and the aces might get you some holes at the end of the play (31-4). Besides, if you lead an ace your opponent can safely play a 5 or a 6. If you lead a 4, he can't, and may be forced to play a face card.
8. Lead the 7. If it gets paired, you score 15-2 with your ace.

Just as playing from a 3-card 11 combination will score 31-2 for the non-dealer whenever dealer plays two ten-cards, a 3-(or 4) card combination totaling 16 will score 31-2 whenever dealer plays a ten-card and a 5. Dealer often has 10's and 5's, so why not take advantage when he does? Here are four examples:

1.

Mia	Woody
6	10 (16)
7 (23)	5 (28)
3 (31-2)	10
5 (15-2)	5 (20-3)

2.

Wally	Theodore
4	J (14)
8 (22)	5 (27)
4 (31-2)	10
3 (13)	Q (23-1)

3.

George	Al
6	K (16)
6 (22)	5 (27)
4 (31-5)	Q
9 (19)	J (29-1)

4.

Moe	Curly
7	Q (17)
7 (24)	5 (29)
A (30)	Go
A (31-4)	J
	K (20-1)

- Once you begin playing from your 16-combination, continue playing from it if dealer plays a ten-card.
- Note that in each hand, non-dealer must put the count above 21 with his second card, forcing dealer to play his 5. Allowing dealer to play two ten-cards (for instance, by leading an ace in hand 4) would eliminate the opportunity to score 31-2. It

can be especially effective if your 16-combination is 3-4-9 or 4-6-6. Lead the 9 from 3-4-9, or a 6 from 4-6-6. If dealer has only ten-cards and 5's, you'll score 31 for 5, as in hand 3.

- Hand 2 contains both an 11-combination (4-4-3), and a 16-combination (4-4-8). It might be wiser to play from the 11-combination, as dealer could have four ten-cards, rather than ten-cards and a 5.
- Finally, note that non-dealer managed to outpeg dealer on each of these hands. There's no guarantee this will happen, but when dealer happens to have ten-cards and 5's you have a good shot at coming out ahead.

Responding to the Opening Lead

Once your opponent's opening lead hits the table, you, as dealer, will first look to see if you can score 15-2. It is seldom dangerous to do so if you can. If you have no 15-2 available, can you pair the opening lead? If so, are you willing to risk the possibility your opponent will triple? Never pairing the opening lead is overly cautious, and will cost you a lot of points. Always pairing is also risky. Leading from a pair is common, and you can expect to pay the price with some frequency if you always pair.

Perhaps the best strategy is to pair the opening lead only when you can peg again if your opponent triples. Holding A-4-Q-K, you can afford to pair your opponent's king, because if he triples, you score 31-2 with your ace. You've lost only two points. If you restrain yourself from pairing on those occasions when you stand to lose four points, you'll make a steady profit in the long run.

When you cannot score 15-2, and cannot (or don't wish to) pair, you still have opportunities to help yourself:

Suppose your opponent has led with a face card. Do you have two cards which total 11? If so, play one of them. If your opponent plays another face card, you score 31-2.

Suppose your opponent has led a 7, and you hold 6-9. Play the 9. If he has an 8, and scores a 3-card run, you get a 4-card run. Likewise, play the 6 if your opponent leads an 8. If he scores a run with a 7, you get a better run with your 9.

If your opponent leads a low card, try to avoid playing a ten-card, as he may well be leading from 2-3 or A-4.

Try to put the count above 15, and below 21, to prevent your opponent from scoring 15-2 or 31-2.

Assume your opponent will peg on any card you play. Play the card that will allow you to score on the card he plays. Here are some examples:

Bart	**You**
7	?

Holding A-2-3-4, play the 3. If opponent scores 15-2 with a 5, you get a 3-card run with your 4. Play anything else and you have no answer to opponent's pegging.

Bart	**You**
4	?

Holding 3-8-9-10, play the 8. If Bart scores 15-2, you can pair his 3. However, holding 2-8-9-10, play the 9. Again you can pair if Bart scores 15-2.

Strategy as Play Progresses

As play progresses, your options become more limited, but your knowledge of your opponent's holding increases. There are a few strategies you may be able to employ. They are:

1. Guessing your opponent's remaining cards

2. Noting the cards your opponent *doesn't* have

3. Setting yourself up for counter-pegging

4. Getting rid of your danger cards

5. The strong finish

6. Controlling the count

7. Watching the suits of the cards

Guessing Opponent's Cards   Each card that your opponent plays is a clue to her holding. Remember, she normally tries to save a good hand. Sometimes she fails, but with six cards to choose from, usually she will manage to have some points. Your job is to guess what cards she might have saved to get those points. This is not an exact science, but if you make educated guesses about her holding, you will sometimes be right, and when you are right, it will often pay off.

Suppose your opponent leads out with a 9. Your hand is 5-6-9-10. Your first guess is that she has a 6 or another 9. You score 15-2 with the 6. This is safer than pairing, and you know that if she pairs your 6, you can score 31-2 with your 10. She plays a deuce. You might now guess that she has a 4 with her 9 and deuce, as 9 + 2 + 4 = 15.

You thus decide not to play the 10, as this would make the count 27. You're also concerned that she might have another 9 (2-4-9-9, perhaps), so you don't play the 5, which would make the count 22. You play the 9. Occasionally this will backfire; she won't have a 4, or a 9, but will have a 5 and will score 31-2. Nonetheless, with nothing better to go on, you may as well try to guess her cards.

Suppose you lead the 8 from A-6-7-8. Your opponent plays a queen. Now what? With nothing better to go on, you might guess he has face cards and 5's. You play the 7, knowing that if he plays a 5, the count will be 30, and your ace will score 31-2. If your hand had been 2-6-7-8, you would play the 6 on opponent's queen, so that if he plays a 5, your *deuce* will score 31-2.

Suppose you hold 3-3-4-5. Your opponent leads a queen and you score 15-2 with your 5. She plays a jack, making the count 25. At this point I would be sorely tempted to "guess" that she is holding 5-10-J-Q, or 10-J-Q-Q, or something similar. I would play a 3, hoping to hear her say "go," so that I can score 31-4 with my other 3. If she is holding 2-3-J-Q, *she* will get the 31-4, but there's a good chance she'd have led the 3 from that hand. If she has 3-J-Q-Q, she will score 31-4, but at least she saved a bad hand.

One word of caution: when guessing an opponent's cards, you may get into trouble if you don't guess *all* of them. Say you hold 2-6-7-9. You lead the 6, the dealer scores 15-2 with a 9, and you pair him. He now scores 31-2 with a 7. Do you play the 7 or the deuce now? You might play the deuce. The dealer has played a 7 and a 9, and it looks like he might have an 8 there. You don't want him scoring 15-2 with it. Or *do* you? What if he has an 8 *and* a 6 or a 9? He'll play the 8 on your deuce, and then score a three-card run with his last card.

Noting Cards Opponent Doesn't Have Although the strategy of watching your opponent's cards and guessing at what he saved can often pay off, it can also backfire when you guess wrong. If your opponent has played 2-3-3, the only cards he's unlikely to have left are a 6 or an 8. If he has played 5-10, his last two cards could easily be 6-7, or 3-4, or 4-6, or K-K, or A-9, or any of a few dozen other possibilities.

In short, figuring out what your opponent *has* is guesswork. But there is a closely related strategy which involves no guesswork at all: figuring out what your opponent *doesn't* have! Say you hold 3-6-6-9. You lead a 6, and your opponent plays a 10. You should now play the other 6, making the count 22. Why? Because if your opponent has the 9 he needs for 31, why didn't he use it to score a 15-2?

Here's another example. Holding 3-4-8-K, you lead the 8. Your opponent plays a queen, you play your king for 28, and he plays a deuce: 30 and a go. Now you must play your 3 or your 4. You note that the opponent has played a queen and a deuce. It looks like he might have a 3 there, so you decide to play your 4. But wait! If he has a 3, why didn't he play it back when the count was 28? You stop yourself just in time, and play the 3, which pays off, as his last two cards turn out to be 4-9.

Anytime your opponent fails to score a 15-2 or a 31-2, or even a run, make a mental note of the card he apparently does not have. You'll find you can use this information to your advantage fairly often.

Setting Up for Counter-Pegging We've seen this strategy in action already, when we led a 4 from 4-7, secure in the knowledge that if the opponent paired our 4, we could score 15-2 with our 7. You needn't be on opening lead to employ this strategy. Suppose the play proceeds as follows:

Bob	You
3	3 (6-2)
10 (16)	?

If your remaining cards are 4-5-7, you would play the 4. If it gets paired, the count is 24, and you peg with your 7. If your remaining cards are A-5-7, you would play the 7. The ace is your insurance, for the count will be 30 if your 7 gets paired.

The lesson: when none of your options looks particularly dangerous, try to choose one that allows you to counter any pegging your opponent might do.

Getting Rid of Danger Cards Your danger cards are 5's. 5's are great to have because they make 15-2's so easily, but they can be dangerous in the pegging, because you may be forced to lead one, giving opponent a 15-2 if he has any face card or 10. Thus, once it appears unlikely that you will score 15-2 with a 5, try to get rid of it. Here's an example:

You	Don
10	K (20)
J (30)	A (31-2)
5	Q (15-2)
5 (20)	4 (24-1)

Had you played one of your 5's on Don's king, you would have avoided the embarrassment of giving him the easy 15-2.

The Strong Finish As you are attempting to peg, your opponent is attempting to prevent you from pegging. When you lead a 4, he is unlikely to play a 2, 3, 5, or 6, as you could score a run. He may even refrain from pairing your 4, fearing that you will triple. This is the type of play you can expect from a good opponent. But as the play progresses, he will have fewer cards from which to choose. When he's down to his last card, he must play it, whether it allows you to score a run or not. Though you don't know what your opponent's last card(s) will be, it often pays to keep, as your last two cards, a pair, or two cards which could work to form a run. We've seen examples of this in the section on tossing to the crib. Let's look at a few more.

1.

Joan	You
10	5 (15-2)
5 (20-2)	K (30)
A (31-2)	10
9 (19)	J (29-4)

By keeping the touching cards (10-J), you maximized your chances of a run. You score a run if Joan's last card is a queen, as well.

2.

Joan	You
K	5 (15-2)
2 (17)	K (27)
3 (30)	Go
A (31-2)	10
	10 (20-3)

Holding onto the pair of 10's until last pays off, as Joan plays all of her cards, leaving you with just the pair.

3.

You	Joan
7	10 (17)
8 (25)	4 (29)
Go	A (30-1)
3	5 (8)
4 (12-4)	

Here we see you needn't be the dealer to score big at the end of the play.

4.

Joan	You
6	9 (15-2)
9 (24-2)	Go
5 (29)	
A (30-1)	10
	10 (20-2)
	10 (30-7)

Lucky you. Joan had to play all of her cards, leaving you with three 10's, which you could play consecutively for a total of nine holes.

EXPERT TIP

Sometimes as the play of the hand progresses, you'll find yourself holding three cards, while an opponent holds only one. This happens whenever you deal, your opponent's second card puts the count over 21, you say, "go," and your opponent plays one more card.

If, among your three remaining cards, you have a pair, you will be tempted to lead from that pair, hoping the opponent will be forced to pair you with his last card and that you can then triple.

Take a look at the following example:

John	You
8	J (18)
6 (24)	Go
7 (31-2)	?

Your remaining cards are Q-Q-K. If John's last card is a king, you are better off playing a queen now. And if John's last card is a queen, you are still better off playing a queen, as you will triple. So you reach for a queen. But wait! Is there any card John might be holding, which would make playing the king a profitable play?

An ace! If John's card is an ace, playing your king will allow you to play your queens consecutively, scoring 31-4, rather than 31-2. Which is John more likely to be holding with 6-7-8? An ace, which improves the hand, or a king or queen, neither of which does? Probably an ace. It can also be argued that if John had a face card, he'd have played it on your jack, hoping for a go.

Here's another example:

John	You
8	J (18)
8 (26)	Go
4 (30-1)	?

Your three remaining cards are 9-9-10. Playing a 9 will pay off if John's last card is a 9 or a 10. And it very well could be. But it looks to me like he might have a 3 there. If so, you'll want to play the 10, which also pays off if John has an ace or a deuce.

To summarize, when holding three cards, including a pair, to your opponent's one card, decide whether your opponent's card is more likely to match your pair, or to be a low card—so low it'll allow you to play your matching cards consecutively. If the low card seems more likely, hang onto your pair.

Controlling the Count You don't have much control over the count, but when none of your other strategies applies, you may have the option of putting the count under 5 or over 15, so that the opponent cannot score a 15-2. You can also put the count under 21 so that the opponent cannot score 31-2.

If you can't put the count in the 0-4 range, or the 16-20 range, it's generally a good idea to make the count as high as possible. This reduces the number of cards with which your opponent can peg. If the count is 20, and you have a 6, 7, and 8, the 8 is more likely to get you a go. Your opponent can score only with an ace, deuce, or 3. Play the 7, and he scores with a 4 as well, and the 6 lets him score with a 5.

There are some cases in which the strategy of making the count as high as possible should be ignored:

1. Don't play the higher card if it gives an opponent a shot at big pegging. For instance, if the count is 25, and you hold a 3 and a deuce, the 3 is a dangerous play, as your opponent may have a 3, and score 31-4. Better to play the deuce.
2. If you like to take a gamble, sometimes you will have the opportunity to score 31-4 *if* you're willing to risk letting your opponent score big. Say the count is 27 and you hold two deuces and a 3. Although the 3 is safer, you might want to gamble that your opponent does not have a deuce, and play one of your deuces. You are hoping the opponent says, "go," allowing you to score 31 for 4. This may seem to contradict the previous suggestion, but here you hold two deuces. This not only reduces the possibility that your opponent has a deuce, it rewards you in those instances that he has no deuce.

Watching the Card Suits At first it may seem that the suits of the cards are irrelevant, unless you happen to have a flush or the right jack. But remember that an opponent may have a flush. If you suspect that he does (a suspicion you'll develop after seeing three of his cards), you may need to make a decision based on the suit of *your* cards. Suppose a hand has played out as follows:

Ted	You
10	K (20)
6 (26)	4 (30)
A (31-2)	?

Your last two cards are the deuce of hearts and the 3 of clubs. You don't expect Ted's last card to be a deuce or a 3, but it *could* be. If all three of Ted's exposed cards are hearts, you would play your deuce. You know that if Ted has a flush, he can't have a deuce with which to pair you, because you have the deuce of hearts. Conversely, if all of Ted's cards are clubs, you would play your 3. Again you fear Ted has a flush, and if he does, he can't have a 3.

Suppose you're playing against me early in the final game of a cribbage tournament. The cut is a 4, and play so far has gone as follows:

Me	You
8	J (18)
6 (24)	5 (29)
2 (31-2)	?

Your remaining cards are 3-7. Which would you play? My guess is that you would play the 3, as I am more likely to have saved 2-6-7-8 than 2-3-6-8. After all, 2-3-6-8 is worth nothing.

But wait! I forgot to tell you that the 2, 6, and 8 I've played are all spades, and so is the cut. You have the 7 of spades and the 3 of diamonds. It occurs to you that I might have saved a flush, and if I did, I can't peg on your 7. My last card *could* be the 3 of spades, however.

You think it over. If I have a 7, my hand is worth seven points. If I have the 3 of spades, my hand is worth twelve points. What seemed like a clear play just a moment ago now seems like a toss-up: 3 or 7,...7 or 3. Finally you play the 7. And I score 15-2 with the 8 of diamonds!

Note that if I'd played the 8 of diamonds on opening lead instead of the 8 of spades, you would not have considered playing the 7. By playing my three spades, and concealing my diamond, I created the illusion I had a flush. I gave you something else to worry about. Perhaps you'd have made the right choice this time, perhaps not, but the lesson to be learned is that the more often you can give your opponent a guess, the more often he will guess wrong. Thus, if you have three cards of the same suit, try to play them first. If your opponent is concerned that you have a flush, he'll be more likely to err when trying to guess your last card.

Strategy on 4th Street

The pegging strategies we've discussed thus far are sound, but they are general strategies, which need to be abandoned occasionally when the situation demands it. On 4th street (the last 30 holes), the position of the pegs may force you to make plays that would seem silly earlier in the game.

It is not useful to discuss 4th street strategy in general; correct strategy on 4th street often depends on the exact position of the pegs, and a slight difference in the position may demand a complete change in tactics. For example, suppose you need two holes to win, and opponent, who needs three, deals. From 4-5-Q-Q you might lead a queen, secure in the knowledge that if dealer pairs or scores 15-2, you have the right card to peg out and win. But suppose the dealer needs only two holes. Now your best lead is the 4, as opponent can peg only with a 4 of his own. If you lead a queen, he pegs out with a 5 or a queen.

You must be prepared to reevaluate the situation after every play you make on 4th street, and perhaps the most useful means of discussing 4th street strategy is to examine a few positions and learn what to think about when the game is on the line.

Position 1:
Both players need 2 holes to win, opponent deals
When the game comes down to a pegging duel on the last hand, the dealer, only two holes from victory, is not likely to bother saving as many points as possible. She does not need them. She knows it's a near certainty that you have enough points to win with first count, so she will put her efforts into pegging those two holes before you

count your hand. She would happily toss 4-6 from 2-4-5-6-7-9, saving no points, because she knows that with 2-5-7-9, she can peg on anything you lead, with the exception of an ace, 3, or 4.

Your best strategy on opening lead, then, will be to lead the card she is least likely to peg on. This is easy enough to determine. Add the number of cards she might be holding that can pair you, to the number of cards she might be holding that can score 15-2. Do this for each of your cards, and lead the card that yields the lowest total. Almost always this will be a low card if you have one. A card lower than a 5 limits your opponent's possible pegging cards, as she can peg only by pairing. Leading anything from 5 through king allows opponent to peg by pairing *or* scoring 15-2.

Sometimes you won't have a low card. You can still play the odds, however. You were dealt six cards, and you've seen the cut. Have you seen any pairs or 15-2's? If so, that's one less pegging card for your opponent to be holding. For example, you are dealt 6-9-10-10-K-K. You save 6-9-10-K. The cut is a 9. And you lead the 6 or the 9. Why? Because to peg on your 6 or 9, your opponent must have a 6 or a 9 of her own. Since you were dealt a 6 and a 9, and the cut was a 9, there are only five more such cards available. If you're lucky, your opponent doesn't have one of them. Had the cut been a 10, your best bet would have been to lead a 10, as this is now the card your opponent is least likely to peg on.

Sometimes you'll have *two or more* cards that seem to give your opponent an equal chance of pegging. For instance, say you are dealt A-4-5-5-6-6. You hold A-4-5-6, and toss 5-6. The cut is a 5. The ace and 4 are equally likely to be paired, so do you choose one at random? You can, but a better policy, since you, like the opponent, need only two holes to win, would be to determine which lead gives you the better chance to peg on your opponent, *if she doesn't peg on you*. If you lead the 4, and the opponent cannot pair, she can play a 2, 7, 8, or 9 to survive. If you lead the ace, and she cannot pair, she must play a 2, 3, or 7 to stay alive. The ace gives you a slightly better chance of winning.

As the play progresses, you can continue playing the odds. Suppose you do lead the ace from A-4-5-6, and your opponent finds one of the safe responses, a deuce, making the count 3. Do you play the 4, 5, or 6 next? If you play the 4, dealer wins with a 3, 4, or 8. If you play the 5, dealer wins with a 5 or a 7. But if you play the 6, dealer can peg only with a 6 of her own, so the 6 is best. Remember, the longer you can prevent dealer from pegging, the more opportunities you'll have to get those two holes yourself.

As in most card games, the proper strategy is perfectly capable of exploding in your face. As an extreme example, suppose you and opponent each need two holes to win. You are leading from 4-4-4-5. Of course you lead a 4. But your opponent's hand turns out to be 3-4-6-6. He pairs your 4 to win. Had you led the 5, you would have pegged on anything he played. Highly annoying. Still, if you consistently play the odds, you'll come out on top more often than not.

Quiz 6

What would you lead from each of these hands, assuming both you and the dealer need two holes to win?

Your Hand	Toss	Cut	Lead
1. 4-7-9-J	3-K	9	____
2. A-2-3-4	3-7	7	____
3. 3-9-9-9	6-9	6	____
4. 2-2-3-3	2-3	K	____

Solutions

1. Lead the 4, preventing dealer from scoring 15-2.
2. Lead the 3, the card dealer is least likely to have.
3. Lead a 9. Dealer can peg only with one of the two remaining 6's; if you lead the 3 he can peg with one of the three remaining 3's.
4. Lead a 3. Either lead allows you to peg on the dealer's first card if that card is an ace, 4, or any ten-card. Leading the 3 also allows you to peg if the dealer plays a 9.

Position 2:
Both players need two holes to win; you deal

As dealer in this position, you once again play the odds. Obviously, if you can peg on opponent's opening lead, you do so. But if you can't peg, play the card your opponent is least likely to peg on. This can mean making plays you might not consider earlier in the game. Suppose the opening lead is an ace. Normally you would refrain from playing a 7, as this would give opponent a shot at 15 for 4 with his own 7. But if your opponent needs only two holes, you happily play the 7, knowing he can peg only with a 7, while any other card gives him at least two different pegging cards.

If your opponent does not lead a low card, and you can put the count in the 16 to 20 range, do so. Opponent can peg two holes only by pairing.

And finally, if you have two equally attractive plays, try to determine whether one of them might give you a better chance of pegging on your opponent's next play.

Quiz 7

Which card would you play on each lead below, assuming that both you and opponent need two holes to win?

Your Hand	Toss	Cut	His Lead	Your Play
1. 2-4-4-K	9-J	8	9	_____
2. 7-8-8-J	8-J	7	9	_____
3. A-6-8-K	7-9	2	3	_____
4. 3-4-5-Q	2-9	K	A	_____

Solutions

1. Play the king. He can peg out only with a king. If you play anything else he pegs out with a 2 or a 4.
2. Play the 7. He can peg only with a 7 or an 8, and since you can see two 7's and three 8's, the odds are with you. If you play the 8 he pegs with a 7, 8, or 10, and if you play the jack he pegs with a 10 or jack. In either case, there are more winning cards available to him.
3. Play the 6. He can peg only with a 6 of his own.
4. Play the 3. The 4 is obviously out of the question. Whether you play the 3, the 5, or the queen, there are two different cards with which your opponent can peg. None is more likely than any other to prevent him from pegging. So choose the one most likely to help you peg. If you play the 3, and he can't peg, he will have to give you a shot at 15-2. You'll win if he plays a 6 or a 7. If you play the queen or the 5, he may put the count over 15, so that you can peg only by pairing.

Position 3:
You need two holes, dealer needs three

The most the dealer can peg with his first card is two holes. Therefore, in this position you can afford to let him peg with his first card, if you get equal counter-pegging.

Simple enough; let's go right to the quiz:

Quiz 8

Which card do you lead from the following hands, assuming you need two holes, and dealer needs three:

Your Hand	Toss	Cut	Lead
1. 2-6-9-9	3-4	3	____
2. 3-7-8-9	5-5	K	____
3. A-5-6-7	K-K	9	____
4. A-4-7-8	5-Q	Q	____
5. A-2-7-8	2-9	J	____

Solutions

1. Lead a 9. Your opponent cannot peg without giving you the game.
2. Lead the 3. Same reason.
3. This time the 7 is completely safe.
4. Both the 4 and the 7 are safe. However, the 4 gives the dealer fewer safe plays, while the 7 allows him to put the count over 15. Lead the 4.
5. The 7 would have been safe, if that jack hadn't been cut. Now the dealer needs only one hole, so play the deuce, the card he's least likely to peg on. An example of how your strategy can change abruptly, even before you've seen any of your opponent's cards.

Position 4:
You deal, with enough points to win—*if* you get to count them

There is one cribbage situation in which you needn't worry about your play backfiring. It's a situation in which the right play can never hurt you, but the wrong play could cost you a game.

Suppose you need five holes to win, and your opponent needs fifteen. You deal, and save 2-3-8-9. The cut is a 4. Your opponent leads out with a 4, and you play your 9, making the count 13. Opponent plays another 4 (17) and your 8 makes the count 25. Now opponent scores a go with a 5.

Opponent	You
4	9 (13)
4 (17)	8 (25)
5 (30-1)	?

Do you play the deuce or the 3?

The key in this situation is to determine how many points the opponent has if he can peg on your play. To peg on your deuce, your opponent must have a deuce of his own. If he has a deuce, his hand is worth 12 points. He has already pegged one hole, and if you play the deuce, he'll peg two more. He'll win the game.

If you play the 3, your opponent can peg only with a 3 of his own. If he has a 3, his hand is worth seventeen points. He *already* has enough points to win. Thus playing the 3 cannot hurt you. Playing the deuce *could* give your opponent the game.

Now let's look at the same hand, but this time, suppose your opponent needs twenty holes to win, instead of fifteen. Should you play the deuce or the 3?

Clearly the worst that can happen if you play the deuce is that your opponent pairs it, but if he does so, his hand is worth only twelve points, not enough to win, even with the points he pegs. But if you play the 3, and his last card is a 3, he has seventeen points, and pegs a total of three holes. He wins the game. Thus playing the 3 could cost you the game, while playing the deuce cannot hurt you at all.

In both cases, your cards are the same, the play of the hand is the same, but because the opponent's position on the board is slightly different, you must play differently to assure that you don't throw away a game you should win. This type of situation, which comes up only near the end of a game, can be much more complicated than the previous example. Nonetheless, by applying logic, you may be able to save many a game. Let's look at a few more of these endgame problems.

If you "think with your hands," it might help to set up the board and cards as you work through the following.

Quiz 9

In each case, assume that you have enough points in your hand and your crib to win—*if* you get to count them.

1.

Your Hand	Cut	He Needs	Him	You
3-5-9-9	K	13	A	9 (10)
			K (20)	9 (29)
			2 (31-2)	?

a) He's already pegged two of the thirteen he needed. Do you play the 3 or the 5?

b) What would you play if he needed 10 holes, instead of 13?

c) Does it matter what you play if he needed 7 holes?

2.

Your Hand	Cut	He Needs	Him	You
4-5-6-10	A	7	Q	6 (16)
			Q (26)	5 (31-2)
			4	?

a) Do you play the 4 or the 10?

b) Which do you play if he needed 10 holes?

c) Which do you play if he needed 13 holes?

d) Which do you play if he needed 16 holes?

3.

Your Hand	Cut	He Needs	Him	You
A-2-2-3	A	13	3	3 (6-2)
			9 (15-2)	2 (17)
			2 (19-2)	?

a) He's already pegged four of the thirteen he needed. Do you play the ace or the deuce?

b) Which do you play if he needed 18 holes?

c) Which do you play if he needed 26 holes?

Solutions

1. a) Normally playing a 5 when the count is 0 is not advisable, but what happens if you play the 5 here? If he can peg on your 5, he has no more than six points. That, plus the total of four he pegs, only adds up to ten, not enough to win. But if you play the 3 and he can pair you, he has nine points, and pegs four. He wins the game!

b) If opponent has a 3, he won the game when he scored 31-2. Thus it can't hurt to play the 3. However, if your opponent has a king or a 5, he has six points, and needs to peg two more. And if you play the 5, he will. Playing the 5 could cost the game.

c) It could matter. Playing the 3 can't hurt, because if it gets paired, you'd have lost the game no matter which card you played, as your opponent has nine points in his hand. But if you play the 5 and your opponent's last card happens to be the right jack, he has three points, and you've given him the holes he needed to win.

Remember, if your opponent can't peg on either of your cards, it doesn't matter what you do. So your only concern is what will happen if he *can* peg on one of your cards. You may lose the game playing the correct card, but you'd have lost anyway. If you lose the game playing the *wrong* card, it is possible you could have won.

2. a) Your opponent has already shown six points. If that's all he has, you can't let him peg anything. If he can peg on your 10, he has an ace or a 10. Either way, he has more than six points, and has won the game, so go ahead and play the 10; it won't affect the outcome. If he can peg on your 4, he may have a 4, in which case he has won, *but he may have a 7!* If so, he needs to peg another hole. Playing the 4 could give him the 15-2 he needs to win the game.

b) If the opponent can peg on your 4, he either has a 4, and will win no matter what you do, or he has a 7, and will lose no matter what you do. It can't hurt to play the 4.

But if you play the 10 and your opponent has a 10, his hand is worth eight points, and you've let him peg the other two he needs.

c) Again the 4 is safe, and again the 10 is dangerous. If the opponent's last card is an ace, he has twelve points, and if you play the 10, he'll score 15-2 and steal the victory from your grasp.

d) Now the victory is safe if you play the 10, for if the opponent pegs on your 10 he cannot move sixteen holes. However, if you play the 4, pairing him, and his last card is a 4, he pegs six holes, and has twelve points, more than enough to pull out the game.

3. a) Play the ace. If he has an A, 2, or 3, you've already lost, but if you play the deuce and he has a ten-card, he scores 31-2, and has seven points. Just enough to win. If you play the ace, he can only get a go with a ten-card, and falls one hole short (unless his ten-card is the right jack).

b) This time either card could lose. If he has a 3, he has fourteen point, and has already won the game and there's nothing you can do about it (of course, if he has a 3, it's hard to believe he didn't play it on *your* 3). However, if he has an ace or a deuce, he has twelve points, and needs to peg two more holes. If he pairs the card you play, he wins. So play the card he's least likely to pair. You can see three deuces, and only two aces, so play the deuce.

c) Play the ace. If he has a deuce, he has twelve points. More than enough to win if you let him peg twelve more holes with his deuce.

Positional Cribbage

Victory does not always go to the player with the best hand. Here's a hand on which you're holding 24 points, needing only one point to win, while the dealer holds absolutely nothing, and needs eight points. But the dealer pegs out, and your 24-hand is wasted:

Your Hand	His Hand	Cut	You	Him
7-7-7-7	3-8-9-K	A	7	8 (15-2)
			7 (22)	9 (31-5)
			7	K (17)
			7 (24)	3 (27-1)

If you've played a few games of cribbage, you've noticed that the player who is behind in the game sometimes has the better chance of winning. If the dealer needs five and the non-dealer needs seven, the non-dealer will usually win. He has the advantage of counting first. If the dealer needs eighteen and the non-dealer needs fourteen, the dealer will usually win. She has the advantage (if her opponent doesn't manage to move fourteen holes) of counting a hand and a crib, and then counting first on the next hand—three hands in a row, plus pegging.

There are positions on 4th street that are advantageous for each player, and if you can reach one of these positions, you'll have an excellent chance of winning. What are these advantageous positions, and how does one improve his chances of reaching one of them?

Non-Dealer The non-dealer would like to be close enough to the game hole so that an average hand (plus pegging) will put him out. An average hand is probably about seven points, and the non-dealer can hope to peg a couple holes, so a position less than ten holes from victory would be cause for slight optimism.

How can you reach this optimum position, less than ten holes from victory? When *dealing* on 4th Street, once the starter card is revealed, you know how many points you have. You know what you threw in your crib, and can make a reasonable guess at whether your crib will be valuable. Are you likely to reach your desired position? If you are going to get there, your best strategy may be to play defensively—to prevent your opponent from pegging. But if it seems likely you *won't* reach a good position, you may wish to play offensively—to take risks in hopes of pegging a few holes.

Dealer The dealer would like to be positioned such that the total points in his hand, his crib, and his next hand (plus pegging) will put him out. One could estimate that the two hands will be worth seven points each, and the crib perhaps four. Add another four to six holes for two hands worth of pegging, and we see that the dealer would like to be less than 25 holes from home.

How can you arrange to be inside this 25-holes-from-victory line? As *non-dealer*, approaching 4th street, determine whether you already have enough points to move inside this line. If so, play defensively. If not, play offensively, for if you fail to peg a few holes, you will need above average cards the rest of the way to win.

When you need to play offensively:

1. Peg at every opportunity, even at the risk of being out-pegged substantially.
2. Save your pairs and touching cards for the end, as we've discussed earlier.
3. Entice your opponent into a run that will lead to pegging on your part. For instance, say the opening lead is a 9. Holding 2-3-4-10 you might play the 10. If your opponent plays an 8 or a jack, scoring three points, you have the right card to score 31-2. Not a good trade-off normally, but if the opponent's position is such that

three points won't help him much, while two points moves you closer to your optimum position, this trade could win you the game. It probably won't, but it *could*. Why not give yourself every edge?

When you need to play defensively:

1. Save a diversity of cards, to avoid getting trapped into a run.

2. Put the count in the 1-4 or 16-20 ranges.

3. Don't score 15-2's, pairs, or runs that could be extended. When the opponent leads a 6, he often has a 9. If you score 15-2, he'll pair you. Better to play a king and hope he can't pair that. Remember, if you've already attained your optimum position, you can focus on preventing your opponent from reaching his.

If you keep your opponent from reaching a good position, but he draws a twenty-point hand, your work was for naught. And if you reach your optimum position, only to draw a two-point hand and a blank crib...oh, well, that's cribbage!

Positional cribbage is somewhat unreliable, as it is based on the likelihood that players will get average cards and, in the short term, you can't count on average cards. But unless you want to enter the last hand or two of a game needing spectacular cards, or needing to deal the opponent a "19 hand," you'll pay close attention to your pegs, and strive to get them into a winning position.

Three General Tips

1. Be a pessimist One of the more obvious pegging tips is to look ahead, not just to the immediate danger that opponent will pair, or score 15-2 or 31-2, but to dangers further down the road.

Holding 6-7-8-8, you would not wish to lead the 6. What if opponent plays a 9, scoring 15-2? Now what? Anything you play gives him a chance at a 4-card run and a "go," and he's outpegged you 7 to 0 in just the first two cards.

Suppose you find yourself holding 2-9-9-10. Would you lead the deuce? You might get away with it, but what if opponent plays an 8? Or, worse yet, a jack?

Before playing a card, think: Is there a card my opponent can play that will put me in an uncomfortable predicament? If there is, chances are he will play it, so consider playing a different card yourself.

2. Assume your opponent is a good player Not necessarily, but probably. When he leads a 3, chances are it wasn't chosen totally at random. Chances are he has a deuce, or another 3. If it's the deuce, he wants you to play a face card. You, suspecting what he's up to, will try to avoid playing the face card. If he has another 3, he wants you to pair him. If you suspect this is the situation, you'll refrain from pairing.

Suppose opponent leads a 7. Does he have another 7? Can you deduce that he probably doesn't have a 2-3 or A-4 combination, as he didn't choose to lead from it?

Obviously your opponent has to play *something*, even when no card seems to have an advantage, but frequently he'll have a reason for his plays, and if you can guess what he's thinking, perhaps you can guess what he's holding. Or at least what he isn't holding.

3. Don't be predictable Over time, you will hold identical or very similar hands. Maybe not in the same game, but certainly in the same evening, if you play enough. Thus it's a good idea to vary your play if you're playing many games with the same opponent.

The 6 is a good lead from 6-9, and the 3 is an excellent lead from 2-3. But if you *always* lead the 6 from 6-9, then whenever you lead a 9, dealer will deduce that you have no 6. If you always lead the 3 from 2-3, dealer will know you have no 3 whenever you lead a deuce. Similarly, if you always lead from your pairs, dealer will refuse to pair your opening lead.

In short, when playing your regular opponents, mix things up a little. The less information dealer has about your hand, the better. And this works both ways; if you notice that your regular opponent is somewhat predictable, use that information.

A Sample Game

It's all well and good to study various strategies, but nothing can take the place of playing the game. Presumably you have a friend with whom you can sharpen your skills. If not, you'll probably want to play online, or look for a cribbage club or a nearby tournament. I'll tell you how to do all of these things shortly.

Of course, the first time you play in a tournament, you may feel some tension, so let's play out a "tournament" game right now. It's me against Lorraine, who is an excellent player. I'll try to convey my thought processes as the game progresses. If we're lucky, some strategies we've been discussing will come up during the course of the game.

If you wish, get out your cribbage board and peg along. We'll supply the hands and plays.

Hand 1

Lorraine deals the cards, and I pick up A-2-4-5-6-8.

If it were my crib, I would toss A-2, hoping to get a 3 from Lorraine, or to cut a 3. Since it's Lorraine's crib, I will toss the 8 and a low card. I choose to toss the deuce, and keep the ace because the ace goes well with my 4. It gets me two points if any face card is cut, and I'll get another two points if Lorraine plays a face card when I lead the 4. I cut the deck, and Lorraine turns up a 10.

		The Play	
My hand	**Cut**	**Me**	**Lorraine**
A-4-5-6	10	4	Q (14)
		A (15-2)	K (25)
		6 (31-2)	J
		5 (15-2)	Q (25-1)

I lead from the A-4 combination, as planned. Lorraine has nothing but face cards, and must watch helplessly as I outpeg her six holes to one.

Had I not led from the A-4 combination, I'd have pegged two fewer holes. The dealer has an advantage in the play of the hand, and you'll seldom outpeg her, but leading from A-4 or 2-3 can often get you off to a good start.

My hand is worth 9 points. Lorraine has J-Q-Q-K, including the right jack, for 11 points. And her crib contains 2-3-4-8, worth another 7. I note that had I tossed A-8, rather than 2-8, Lorraine would have had only four points in the crib. The ace is a better defensive toss, as it can form a run only with 2-3, while the deuce can form a run with A-3 *or* 3-4. Keeping the ace did get me extra points in the play and in my hand, however.

Lorraine has a 4-hole lead as I deal for the first time.

Hand 2

I deal myself 3-4-4-7-10-10. Not much of a hand. I toss the pair of 10's into my crib. At least I'll have something there. My hand has potential, but there are many cuts that will leave me with the 4 points I'm starting with. Lorraine cuts, and I turn up an 8.

I'd have preferred a 5, as it would have helped both my hand and my crib, but I can hardly complain. The 8 has improved my hand significantly.

		The Play	
My hand	Cut	Lorraine	Me
3-4-4-7	8	10	7 (17)
		J (27)	4 (31-2)
		Q	4 (14)
		5 (19)	3 (22-4)

As soon as Lorraine's 10 hits the table, I reach for my 7, hoping she'll play another 10-card, and let me score 31-2 with my 11-combination. And my hopes are realized. Not only that, I am left with 3-4, which pays off when Lorraine's last card is a 5. Any touching cards have a chance of getting you a run at the end of the play, depending on opponent's last card, but that last card is often a 5, so try holding onto 3-4, 4-6, or 6-7.

Lorraine has 5-10-J-Q, worth 9 (wrong jack), and my hand is worth 10 points. I flip over my crib to find A-6-10-10, worth another 4 points, and a 7 point lead.

Hand 3

Lorraine deals the third hand, and I pick up 3-4-8-8-J-Q. I don't like tossing touching cards in her crib, as she's got a good chance of getting a run, but the alternative is to save only 2 points, so I toss J-Q. I cut the deck, and Lorraine turns over a 5. Not what I wanted to see after that toss.

| | | The Play | |
My hand	Cut	Me	Lorraine
3-4-8-8	5	8	7 (15-2)
		4 (19)	4 (23-2)
		8 (31-2)	5
		3 (8)	3 (11-3)

I start with an 8, hoping Lorraine will pair it. Some players try to avoid pairing, fearing the triple, but sometimes there's little choice. Holding 8-9-10-10, chances are Lorraine would pair my 8. When she scores 15-2, I play my 4, knowing that if she pegs on that, I'll get equal counter-pegging with my 8.

Note Lorraine's play of the 5. Normally one doesn't make the count 5, but Lorraine could see my 4-8-8, and decided I was more likely to have a 3 than a 5 or a face card. Though it's true that a 5 would not have helped my hand, I might easily have kept one, merely to avoid tossing it in Lorraine's crib, but in this instance she guessed right.

My hand is worth 9 points. Lorraine has 3-4-5-7, worth 12 points, and her crib contains A-A-J-Q (wrong jack), worth another 6. She's pulled back ahead by seven holes.

Hand 4

My fourth hand consists of the following cards: 2-3-4-6-8-9.

It's my crib, and while 6-8 or 8-9 may have the potential to become a bigger crib than 6-9, 6-9 is two points. A bird in the hand. I've had enough blank cribs to have learned that when you can put two points in, you put them in. The cut is a 5.

My hand	Cut	The Play	
		Lorraine	**Me**
2-3-4-8	5	K	8 (18)
		Q (28)	2 (30-1)
		J	4 (14)
		5 (19)	3 (22-4)

I play my 8 on Lorraine's king, hoping to score 31-2 with my 3 if Lorraine plays another face card. She does play another face card, but as I reach for my 3, it occurs to me that she might have a 5 with her face cards. Abandoning my "bird in the hand" attitude, I hold onto my 3-4 hoping for a run at the end. My deuce gets me a go, instead of 31-2, costing me one point, but the sacrifice pays off. Lorraine plays a jack, and I play my 4 (a better play than the 3, as I know she doesn't have an ace with which to score 15-2). She does have a 5, and I get my three card run.

Lorraine has 17 points (5-J-Q-K, wrong jack). This is the third hand out of four on which she's had face cards. A bit unusual, but I dealt two of the three hands myself, so I can't complain about bad shuffling. My hand is worth 8. I turn up the crib and find A-6-8-9, for another 6 points.

Hand 5

I now trail Lorraine by 5 holes, and it's her crib. She deals me A-2-3-9-10-K. I have the option of keeping 2-3-10-K, or A-2-3 and another card. Saving A-2-3 gets me a better hand if a low card is cut, and won't cost much if a high card is cut. You tend to have more potential if you save a run.

Should I keep the 9, the 10, or the king? Not the king, that gives Lorraine 9-10 in her crib. Keeping A-2-3-9 will pay off slightly if a 6 is cut, but 9-K is a safer toss, as Lorraine could toss 5-J, and I would undoubtedly cut her a queen if she did. I cut the deck and Lorraine turns up a deuce.

		The Play	
My hand	Cut	Me	Lorraine
A-2-3-10	2	2	6 (8)
		3 (11)	7 (18)
		A (19)	A (20-2)
		10 (30)	A (31-2)

The play is fairly uneventful for a change. I normally lead the 3 from 2-3, as it gives opponent fewer safe plays. However, the cut was a deuce, which means Lorraine is less likely to have a deuce with which to pair me. Note my play of the ace when the count was 18, keeping the count in the safe 16-20 range. Had I played the 10, Lorraine would have been able to triple my ace.

My hand is worth fourteen points, and Lorraine has A-A-6-7, worth six. Her crib contains 3-4-9-K, and grew from zero to seven points with the deuce I cut for her.

Hand 6

I now trail Lorraine by eight holes. My new hand is 7-8-9-10-J-Q. An easy decision, as it's my crib. I toss the J-Q. If it were Lorraine's crib, I'd toss 10-Q, to keep from giving her touching cards. Lorraine cuts, and I turn up a 3. Not what I was hoping for.

My hand	Cut	The Play	
		Lorraine	**Me**
7-8-9-10	3	4	9 (13)
		K (23)	8 (31-2)
		Q	7 (17)
		A (18)	10 (28-1)

Any of my cards appears safe on Lorraine's lead of a 4. I reject the 10 because she could be leading from A-4 (she was!). I choose the 9 because it allows me to score 31-2 if she plays a face card. The 8 gives me the same advantage, but I hold onto the 7-8, hoping for a "big finish."

The play could proceed:

Lorraine	Me
4	9 (13)
2 (15-2)	10 (25)
3 (28)	Go
2 (30-1)	8
	7 (15-3)

OR

Lorraine	Me
4	9 (13)
2 (15-2)	10 (25)
3 (28-1)	8
6 (14)	7 (21-4)

For once, I have guessed right. Note that if I play anything other than the 9 on Lorraine's 4, the pegging duel could end in a 1 to 1 tie, or with me up 2 to 1. These few extra holes may not matter, but if I win this game by a hole or two, this hand may have been the difference.

Lorraine's hand is worth four points, and mine is worth six. I turn up the crib, finding 3-8-J-Q. It's the right jack, giving me three nice points, and tying the game at 91.

Hand 7

We're both thirty holes from victory. Thirty is a long way to go for Lorraine. She'll be counting three hands in a row, after I count my hand, but she'll still need above average cards to pull out the win. I need to move about eight or ten holes this hand to reach a good position, but my first priority will be to prevent Lorraine from pegging any more than necessary.

My hand is 2-3-4-8-9-J. I toss Lorraine the 8-J, and the cut is a queen.

| | | The Play | |
My hand	Cut	Me	Lorraine
2-3-4-9	Q	3	5 (8)
		9 (17)	6 (23)
		2 (25)	4 (29-1)
		4	Q (14-1)

I have no trouble resisting the bait Lorraine throws my way when she plays her 5 on my 3. If I'd used my 4 to score a 3-card run, she'd have gotten a run of her own, and she needs the points more than I do.

My hand is worth seven points. Lorraine has eleven. She turns up the crib, and finds 2-3-8-J, worth four points. She didn't quite reach her desired position (she needs thirteen), while I barely managed to get to mine (I need 23).

Hand 8

I deal the cards and pick up 6-7-8-9-K-K. The 6-7-8-9 are all hearts, a nice bonus. I toss the kings, pleased to know there'll be something in my crib. Hope I get to count it.

I couldn't have asked for a much better hand. I have a dozen points before the cut, and several chances to improve the hand. Lorraine cuts, and I turn up the 10 of hearts.

There's nothing I can do if Lorraine has thirteen points, so I'll assume fewer, and try to keep her from pegging.

		The Play	
My hand	**Cut**	**Lorraine**	**Me**
6-7-8-9	10	J	8 (18)
		5 (23)	7 (30-1)
		J	?

Lorraine's hand is looking pretty good. She's showing nine points already (including the right jack). I must now play my 6 or my 9. Which is better? Let's figure it out.

If Lorraine can't peg on either of my cards, it doesn't matter what I play. If she can peg on my 6, she has a 6, and her hand is worth nine points. Not quite enough to win, even with the two holes she would get for pairing my 6. If she can peg on my 9, she has either a 9 or a 10. If she has a 9, she has fifteen points; if she has a 10, she has thirteen points. Either way, she already has enough to win, whether I let her peg or not. Thus it can't hurt to play the 9. Playing the 6, while it won't lose me the game immediately, could give Lorraine two valuable points. I play the 9, and Lorraine's last card is a 6! The complete hand:

		The Play	
My hand	**Cut**	**Lorraine**	**Me**
6-7-8-9	10	J	8 (18)
		5 (23)	7 (30-1)
		J	9 (19)
		6 (25)	6 (31-4)

It's interesting to note that if Lorraine had played her second jack on my 8, she might well have pegged enough to win. She couldn't know that, of course. If my hand had been 3-7-7-8, playing the second jack would have allowed me to peg seven holes.

Lorraine pegs her nine holes, coming up four short of victory. I have fourteen, and I pegged five. All I need is four more in the crib. Is that too much to ask? I turn up A-8-K-K. No help from Lorraine. I'm two holes short.

Hand 9

I'm disappointed, but I'm in pretty good shape. I need two holes to win, Lorraine needs four, and I have first count. Lorraine deals and I pick up A-3-6-9-9-K.

I will be saving the 6-9, of course. I need two points, just in case no one pegs out, and 6-9 is better than 9-9, as it gives me an extra choice during the pegging. I decide to keep A-3-6-9. The 3 will be an excellent lead. If it gets paired, my 9 puts me out. The 6 is equally safe, but I prefer the 3 because dealer will feel safe playing a face card on my 6. On the 3 she may fear that I've led from 2-3, and try to play something other than a face card—a 6 or a 9, hopefully.

I cut the deck, and Lorraine turns up…a jack! Yikes! It's a good thing I didn't let Lorraine pair my 6 at the end of the last hand, or this cut would have won the game for her. Lorraine moves within two holes of home.

At this point, I must re-think my strategy. The 3, which was a perfectly safe lead a moment ago, is now no safer than the ace (though still safer than the 6 or the 9). Lorraine is as likely to have a 3 as an ace; therefore, my lead will depend on which card gives me the best chance of pegging *if she can't pair me*.

If I lead the 3 I will peg out on Lorraine's first card if she plays a deuce (unlikely), ace, 6, or 9. If I lead the ace I will peg out if Lorraine plays a deuce, 3, 5, 6, 8, or 9. My choice seems clear.

My hand	Cut	The Play	
		Me	**Lorraine**
A-3-6-9	J	A	7 (8)
		?	

Lorraine plays a 7 on my ace, an excellent play, as it means I can peg only with a 7 of my own. Any other card would have given me two potential pegging cards. I can play the 3, 6, or 9 on her 7. If I play the 6, she can win with a 5, 6, or 8 (also an ace, but she obviously doesn't have an ace). If I play the 3, she can win with a 3 or a 4. If I play the 9 she wins with an 8 or a 9. Since I was dealt two 9's, and one 3, the odds slightly favor playing the 9, and I do. Lorraine plays a deuce, and the count is 19. Do I play the 3 or the 6?

My hand	Cut	The Play	
		Me	**Lorraine**
A-3-6-9	J	A	7 (8)
		9 (17)	2 (19)
			?

Again I'll play the odds. If I play the 3, Lorraine wins with a 3, 4, 7, or 8 (also an ace or a 9, but I know she has neither). If I play the 6, she can win with a 4, 5, or 6 (the 4 and the 5 get her a go, and she'll get another go with her last card). She has more winning plays on my 3, so I play the 6.

Lorraine immediately plays a 3, making the count 28, and I pair her to win. Her other card was a 10.

There are reasonable sequences of play on these same cards that would lead to a win by Lorraine. I was lucky I didn't find any reason to play my 3 before she played hers. And I needed every point I scratched out from the very beginning. Sometimes you play well, and pick up a hole here, a couple more there, but win or lose by twenty. It's when the game is decided by a few holes that the effects of your good plays (and your bad) are magnified.

Game Variations

Cribbage is a great game, but when you have more than two people, or when you want to spice things up a bit, try one of these other forms of cribbage.

Doubles Cribbage

You need four players for doubles, but you need only one cribbage board, as you play with a partner. You sit across from your partner, and one of you is in charge of keeping score. Each player receives five cards, and tosses one into the crib. With 16 cards available during the play of the hand, you'll find there's a lot more pegging. But with only five cards dealt to each player, you'll also find it more difficult to come up with a good hand.

Captain

This is a good way to play three-handed. Two players are teammates. The third is the "captain." The captain gets to start in the 60 hole. That's a big lead, but the others have a good chance of catching up before the end. Each player gets five cards and tosses one, and one card is dealt into the crib.

Reverse Cribbage

The object of this hilarious game is to lose. The first player to reach the game hole loses, so break up your runs, toss your 5's in your opponent's crib, and try for those "19" hands. The crib is usually the best hand at the table.

Solitaire

Deal six to yourself, and two to the crib. Put the deck down, and toss two cards from your hand to the crib (try to toss good ones, because the crib is always yours). Now turn up the top card as your starter. Score your hand and crib, then put the starter card on the bottom of the deck. Repeat. When you're down to the last four cards, that's your last hand. Shuffle the rest of the deck, and cut your last starter. The object is to go out (121) in one pass through the deck. A tough game to win; be happy if you merely escape a skunk.

Football

Each cribbage player gets an opposing team in a televised football game. While you're playing cribbage and watching the game, anytime your football team scores any points, you score that amount on the cribbage board. Anytime your football team turns the ball over, you jump your front peg over your back one. No tackling!

Three Reasons
Why You Will Continue
to Lose Cribbage Games
(even after reading this book)

1. Your opponent gets better cards than you do, seeming to have an inexhaustible supply of 5's and double runs. You, however, regularly draw hands like A-3-7-9-J-K or 2-4-6-8-10-Q.
2. Your opponent gets better cuts than you do. You save 7-7-9-9, he saves 4-4-6-6, and the cut is a 5. Next hand you save 4-4-6-6, he saves 7-7-9-9, and the cut is an 8!

Above are the two *main* reasons. Good cards and good cuts will usually outperform good strategy. But even when the cards are running fairly even, and you get your fair share of good cuts, you still won't always win, because...

3. Almost every pegging strategy we've learned is *certain* to backfire some of the time. Choose any four cards, and there are sure to be four cards your opponent can hold that will allow her to outpeg you. And she *will* hold those four cards some of the time.

What card would you play from the following hand, on opening lead: 2-3-3-Q? Probably a 3, hoping for a 15-2, or even a triple. But the pegging could go:

You	Opponent
3	3 (6-2)
3 (9-6)	3 (12-12)
9 (21)	9 (30-3)
2	2 (4-3)

Outpegged by 14 holes! What would have happened if you had led with the 9?

It might have gone:

You	Opponent
9	9 (18-2)
2 (20)	2 (22-2)
3 (25)	3 (28-2)
3 (31-8)	3 (3-1)

This time you win the pegging duel by one hole—a 15-hole difference. Of course, leading the 9 doesn't work so well if the opponent's 9 is replaced with a 6:

You	Opponent
9	6 (15-2)
3 (18)	3 (21-2)
3 (24-6)	3 (27-12)
2 (29)	2 (31-4)

Outpegged by 14 holes again!

Clearly the success of your pegging strategies will always depend on two things: the cards your opponent holds, and the order in which the cards are played. And unless you can see through the backs of your opponent's cards, you can't be certain in which order to play yours. This can be extremely frustrating, but let's face it: the game would be far less interesting if strategies were foolproof.

So don't be discouraged by your 10-game losing streaks, by the staggering margins of victory your novice opponent enjoys against you, by the humiliating double-skunks you endure. Play the odds: by sticking with the strategies we've learned, using your common sense, and tossing a pair of 5's in your crib now and then. In the long run, you'll come out on top more often than not.

The American Cribbage Congress

Now that you've honed your cribbage skills, you may want to test yourself against some of the better players in your area, or even in the country. Unlike such games as chess, bridge, and golf, in which you would have little chance against the world's best, you could actually have some success at a cribbage tournament. Why?

Because the winner of any individual game is often the player who is dealt the better hands and gets the luckier cuts. The best cribbage player in the world can't beat you if you keep getting 20-point hands and he keeps getting 2-point hands. Besides, your average mathematical genius knows he can't win all the time at cribbage, so he plays a different game. The people who attend cribbage tournaments are people just like you. But, how do you find cribbage tournaments?

In 1979, a group of avid players attending the National Open Cribbage Tournament, in Raleigh, NC, founded the American Cribbage Congress, a non-profit organization whose goals were, and still are, to promote cribbage, to standardize the rules of the game, and to provide a venue for players through organized clubs and tournaments.

The ACC sanctions about 200 tournaments throughout the U.S. each year. The schedule of tournaments appears in *Cribbage World*, a monthly publication sent to each ACC member. To look into joining, dial 1-888-PEGGING for the up-to-date address and cost. You can also log on to www.cribbage.org for membership information, along with strategy tips, cribbage history, tournament schedules, and much more.

If you've never played in a tournament, the prospect may be somewhat intimidating but it shouldn't be. You'll meet new friends, have fun, and with a lucky run of cards, you may even win some money. Here's what to expect:

Most tournaments draw from a few neighboring states, though the most prestigious ones attract players from throughout the country. Tournaments usually run two days, Saturday and Sunday. The formats can differ, but in most cases you'll play 20 games against 20 opponents, and the top fourth of the field will qualify to play off in head-to-head matches, while the rest can play in the consolation tournament. Entry fees vary, but the money comes back to the players in prize money and lunch.

As you might guess, when dozens of cribbage players are playing hundreds of games, irregularities can occur. For instance, what happens when it is discovered, after the play of the hand, that there are too many or too few cards in the crib? What happens if a player pegs into the game hole, but doesn't actually have enough points to get there? What happens if you say "Go," but after your opponent plays his next card, you realize you had a playable card? What happens if you accidentally move your opponent's pegs, or move your own pegs backward?

Resolving such incidents may be easy when playing a buddy at home, but with tournament prize money on the line, it helps to have rules to deal with any irregularity. The ACC's rule book covers just about any possible problem, and is updated periodically. Volunteer judges enforce the rules whenever there is a dispute at a tournament.

If you seek something a bit more casual than a major tournament, the ACC also runs so-called "Grass Roots" clubs in numerous towns and cities. Players meet weekly for mini-tournaments of nine games each. If there's no such club in your area, the ACC will help you create one.

Whether you start out at a Grass Roots club, or brave the tournament trail, the ACC provides a means to hone your game against a wide variety of opponents.

Cribbage on the Computer

Another way to challenge new opponents is to play online. Several online computer services offer the opportunity to play people around the world from the comfort of your own home. Two of the largest are the Microsoft Gaming Zone and Yahoo Games. All you do is download the cribbage program from the web site. Then you can log on anytime and find opponents. Some sites maintain ranking systems, and provide separate rooms for beginners, intermediates, and experts.

To play cribbage online, try these sites:

        www.zone.com
        www.yahoo.com
        www.gametropolis.com
        www.igames.com
        www.playsite.com

Once you reach the home pages of these sites, you'll have to find your way to the cribbage area, but it's not difficult.

If you'd rather not play someone else online, you can still play against the computer. There are many cribbage software programs, and if you can't find one in your local store, the ACC web site will direct you to some good ones.

So, with tournaments, clubs, interactive sites, software, and all your friends available, what are you waiting for? Start pegging!

Cribbage Terms

The terminology of cribbage varies slightly from region to region, and player to player. Some players refer to the "cut," others to the "starter card." Some refer to the "right jack," others to "his nobs." Here are some terms that appear in this book, or that you'll hear spoken by your fellow players.

crib   the hand formed by the players' discards. Scored by the dealer after all other hands have been scored.

cut   refers to the starter card, on top after the cutting of the deck.

dead hole   the last hole before going out; 120 holes from the start. Also called the "stink hole."

double run   a three- or four-card run, with one of the cards paired. For example, 10-J-Q-Q.

double skunk   a victory by 61 or more holes.

go   stated by a player who cannot play any of his cards without putting the count above 31.

muggins   an optional rule that allows one player to score points that the opponent was entitled to, if the opponent fails to score those points himself.

19 hand   universal cribbage lingo for a no-point hand, so called because 19 is the one score you can't get (below 25).

nibs   a jack turned up as the starter card. Also called "his heels."

nobs the jack the same suit as the starter card. It's worth 1 extra point when counting your hand or your crib.

pone short for "opponent," but usually refers to the non-dealer. Each hand has a dealer and a pone.

right jack the jack of the same suit as the starter card, also called his nobs (see above).

run three or more cards in sequence.

skunk a victory by 31 or more points.

starter card the card that is turned up before the start of play, and which becomes a part of each hand and the crib when scoring the points in the hands. It may also be referred to simply as the "cut."

street thirty holes. 1st Street consists of the first thirty holes (outside row); 2nd Street consists of holes 31 to 60 (inside row); 3rd Street consists of *next* 30 holes (the outside street, second time around); 4th Street is the last 30 holes (inside row, second time around), which leads to the game hole.

touching cards two cards that are numerically consecutive. 6-7, for instance, or 10-J.

tripling playing the third consecutive card of the same rank. You lead a 4, opponent pairs your 4, and you play the third 4. You have tripled.

Index

About the Author

Dan Barlow has wasted a good portion of his life playing games, especially bridge, Diplomacy, and cribbage. He won the National Open Cribbage Tournament in 1980, and has had other strong finishes in this tournament. A long-time contributor to *Cribbage World* magazine, his strategy articles now appear on the web pages of both the American Cribbage Congress, and the Microsoft Gaming Zone.

Dan attended the University of North Carolina at Chapel Hill, and still lives in North Carolina with his wife, Jennifer, and son, Stephen. His hobbies, besides games, include ballroom dancing, science fiction, guitar, and racquetball.

For Canadians, contact:

Mensa Canada Society, 329 March Road
Suite 232, Box 11
Kanata, Ontario, Canada, K2K 2E1
(613) 599–5897
info@canada.mensa.org

If you do not live in the U.S. or Canada and would like
to get in touch with your national Mensa, contact:

Mensa International, 15 The Ivories,
6–8 Northampton St.,
Islington, London N1 2HY England
MensaInternational@mensa.org